Animals

in their

Homes

Author: Sonia Goldie

Graphic Design and Illustrations: Pascale Estellon and Anne Weiss

Translated from the French by Eric Bye

10 9 8 7 6 5 4 3 2 1

Published by Lark Books, A Division of
Sterling Publishing Co., Inc.
387 Park Avenue South, New York, NY 10016

Original Title: Maisons des Animaux
Originally published by Mila Editions – France
©1998, Mila Editions

English translation copyright © 2006 by Lark Books

Distributed in Canada by Sterling Publishing, c/o Canadian Manda Group,
165 Dufferin Street, Toronto, Ontario, Canada M6K 3H6
Distributed in the United Kingdom by GMC Distribution Services,
Castle Place, 166 High Street, Lewes, East Sussex, England BN7 1XU
Distributed in Australia by Capricorn Link (Australia) Pty Ltd.,
P.O. Box 704, Windsor, NSW 2756 Australia

Manufactured in China
All rights reserved

ISBN 13: 978-1-57990-920-8
ISBN 10: 1-57990-920-5

For information about custom editions, special sales, premium
and corporate purchases, please contact Sterling Special Sales
Department at 800-805-5489 or specialsales@sterlingpub.com.

Cozy and Safe in Secret Places

Animals need shelters to protect them from cold, rain, and predators. They need places of their own to store food, rest, and raise their little ones in peace.

To make their homes, some animals dig in the dirt with their shovel-like paws. Some build houses in trees with scissor-like beaks. Others carry their houses on their backs.

Animal homes are delicate and precious. If you find one, leave it alone. Every creature has a right to its own safe hiding place.

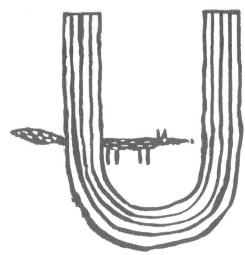 nderground Houses

Who wants to live underground? Lots of animals do.
It's warm and safe down there, faraway from the noise
and light of the outside world. Animals that dig dens
and tunnels underground are called burrowers.

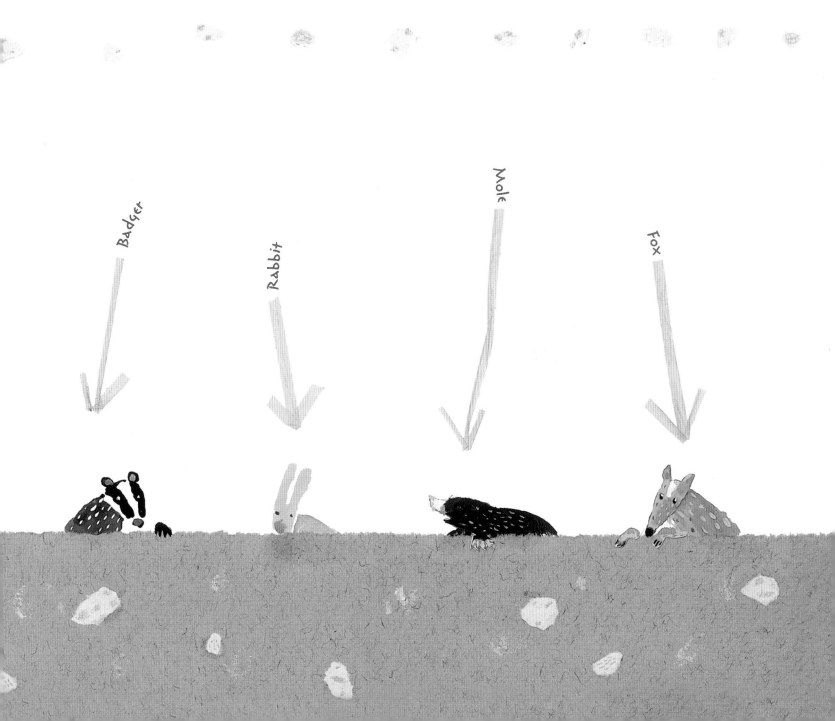

Mole Tunnels

The mole digs underground with its shovel-shaped paws, making a large maze of tunnels. As it digs, the mole eats all the earthworms it comes across.

The mole sets up a storeroom in one part of its maze. In this room, it keeps hay, leaves, and other interesting things that it finds outside.

Even though the mole feels safe in the tunnels, it builds an emergency exit— just in case!

Finished at last!

Almost done!

Yum! A nice, fat earthworm.

A cozy little nest.

Shh! The babies are sleeping.

The storeroom.

The mole spends most of the day in its tunnels and only comes out at night.
Out of sight, out of danger.

All Kinds of Burrows

RABBIT BURROW

NURSERY

Rabbits dig long burrows that they share with other rabbits. When baby rabbits are born, the mother rabbit chooses her own small part of the tunnel to use as a nursery.

The nursery is lined with leaves. Every time the mother rabbit has to leave her babies to find food, she protects them by closing the entrance to the nursery with some dirt.

BADGER'S BURROW

FOX'S DEN

The badger's burrow is very large, comfortable, and tidy. Its rooms are upholstered with moss, ferns, and leaves. The badger changes this lining often and uses only a special part of the burrow as a bathroom.

The fox often takes over an abandoned badger or rabbit burrow. All the fox has to do before moving in is dig out the burrow a little so that it is fox-sized.

Tree Houses

Birds are good at finding what they need to build houses. They make nests out of mud, small pieces of wood, thread, fur, hair, lichen, and twigs.

The natural building materials that birds choose blend in with their surroundings to help keep nests safe and secret.

Creating a nest for a bird family takes a lot of work and skill. Birds know to use small feathers, sheep's wool, and soft moss to line their nests so they stay warm and snug.

Most nests are round, but they come in many other shapes too.

Goldcrest

Owl

Squirrel

Oriole

Woodpecker

The **Baltimore oriole** lives near farms. It collects cow hair and bits of string and uses them to make a pouch-shaped nest. The oriole can even tie a knot to hang its nest from a branch.

The tiny **goldcrest** builds a round hammock-like nest high up in the branches of conifer trees.

Some **owls** like to nest in holes in trees.

The **squirrel** lives as high up in the trees as possible. It weaves a basketlike nest out of twigs in a hole or between two branches. Then, the squirrel adds a cushion of moss. Sometimes, the squirrel spends several days sleeping in its nest. When the squirrel gets hungry, it climbs down to look for hazelnuts, walnuts, acorns, and other food it has buried at the foot of the tree.

Long-Tailed Titmouse

Weaver Finch

Squirrel

Woodpecker

Woodpeckers peck holes in old tree trunks. Using their very strong, scissor-like beaks, they hollow out little rooms for themselves with round doors and smooth walls. To make the rooms comfortable, woodpeckers put wood shavings on the floor.

The **weaver finch** weaves an amazing nest out of dried grasses. Its house is built with little stitches, loops, and knots.

The **long-tailed titmouse's** nest blends in with the tree trunk. Inside, the titmouse makes soft walls with moss, lichen, and spider webs. Then, it lines the whole nest with feathers. The titmouse's nest must be the coziest of all.

Unusual Nests

The warbler sews its nest. It finds a large, rolled-up leaf and pokes holes along the edge. Then, the warbler uses plant fibers like thread to sew the leaf together.

The house martin is a potter. It uses a sticky paste of saliva and mud to build its house in the corner of a wall or under a ledge. Some people believe that you will have good luck if a pair of martins builds a nest on your home.

Surprising Shelters

The stork often lives on chimney tops. It builds a huge nest lined with newspapers and rags to keep its babies comfortable.

The reed warbler is a basket weaver. It attaches a large, basketlike nest to reeds, where the wind rocks it back and forth. A soft, fluffy carpet of flowers and feathers fills the inside of the nest.

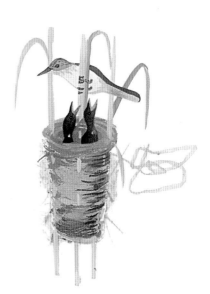

# Houses on the Water

A comfortable den tucked under the roots of a tree, a lodge with the view of the river, a little island house—for animals that can swim, the water's edge provides perfect homes.

Beaver's Lodge

Crested Grebe on Its Nest

Otter's Bed

The crested grebe lives in a swamp. This bird makes its nest with things it collects from the water such as old pieces of wood, water lilies, and other plants. The grebe piles up what it finds to form an island.

The bird watches the level of the river closely. If the water rises, the grebe must build its island nest higher so it will stay above the water. If the water goes down, the bird must be careful because its home will stick out like a little mountain and be easy for predators to see.

Clever Homes

The beaver uses the skills of a woodcutter, mason, and carpenter to build its lodge. Made of wood and branches, the beaver's home is held together with mud and strengthened with stones.

The beaver wants a pond to surround its home. If there isn't enough water to live in, the beaver makes a pond by building a dam.

The entrance to its house is underwater. When the beaver goes in, it wipes its feet in a special little room so that its bed of soft wood shavings won't get wet.

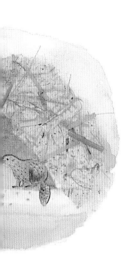

The otter's bed is made of rushes  and reeds. It's tucked out of sight at the edge of the water.

To hide its babies, the otter digs special rooms into the bank. These rooms have underwater entrances and tree root roofs. The caring mother also makes air holes and emergency exits for her babies.

arry Along Homes

What could be more practical than always carrying your house with you? You could rest or hide inside whenever you wanted.

For animals who wear their homes on their backs, finding shelter is never any trouble.

The turtle can go inside its home anytime. All it has to do is pull its legs, head, and tail under its scaly, bony shell.

A baby turtle's shell is very soft. But, as the turtle grows up, its shell becomes hard enough to protect it from predators and heat.

Shell Houses

The hermit crab is born without any protection. So, it moves into someone else's abandoned shell. When it outgrows this shell, the hermit crab looks for another to live in.

It often chooses a shell with small sea anemones attached. The anemones provide even more protection for the hermit crab by stinging anything that comes close.

A snail's spiral shell grows along with it. But, the shell isn't a secure hiding place. Predators can break it and the sun can dry out the snail, even when it's inside the shell.

So the snail hides beneath stones for additional shelter. In the winter, the snail stays underground.

Stickers and Posters

Now that you know all about animal homes, have fun playing with the sitckers and posters at the front of this book.

Put the animal stickers on the posters where you think they should live. Then move them around so the animals can try out new homes.

Puzzle and Maze

While you've been reading, the moles have been busy digging, digging, digging. Would you like to help them?

In the activity kit, you'll find a mole tunnel puzzle. Mix up the pieces, and then connect all the tunnels.

Next, help the moles find their way through the incredible maze!

"I think I could turn and live with animals, they are so placid and self-contained,
I stand and look at them long and long."

~ Walt Whitman